The Drawings of
PAUL DELVAUX

The Drawings of
PAUL DELVAUX

GROVE PRESS

Preface
by
Maurice
Nadeau

Translated by Helen R. Lane

"The overflowing of dreams into real life . . ." How could anyone fail to think of this formula, so characteristic of Gérard de Nerval, on looking at the drawings of Paul Delvaux? From century to century, from poet to painter, there thus sometimes exist troubling fraternities, illuminating relays whereby the world proves to be more mysterious than we thought, richer in unexpected encounters, rustling with harmonies. How have we allowed our universe of slamming doors—so soon closed on childhood, on the confused and crazy desires of adolescence—little by little to screen off these realms that open on boundless perspectives? The moment we begin to follow in the footsteps of Paul Delvaux, we discover a planet whose gravitational pull gives our gestures a different weight. Outside of time, outside of our everyday sense of self, we are astonished to have crossed so easily the boundaries that life imposes on us, boundaries that (curiously enough) are said to be natural. We have perhaps merely returned to that fleetingly glimpsed country that leaves *unsettling lights* in the eyes of the waking sleeper.

It is the rare artist who is at home in this place that is situated elsewhere. Beyond the fact that it requires a *grace* to which very few are ready to abandon themselves, it is not easy to discover, beneath the tangled brambles of life, the paths that lead to it. When a cliff of words, welded to each other by age-old usage, looms up before the poet, his wretchedness has no equal except that of the painter who has wandered into the tangled network of lines, forms, and colors that go to make up the myriad ways of painting before he came on the scene. After straying innocently into this labyrinth, how can it be gotten out of? The rage that overcomes Paul Delvaux when, as a student at the Brussels Academy, one of his fellow students tells us, he finds himself confronted with such ridiculous subjects as "the first swallows" or "the four seasons" and replies with "The Taking of Alesia by the Romans," painted, we are also told, "in a paroxysm of savage fury," this rage, which is a surprise in a gentle, not very communicative adolescent, is traceable less to the helplessness of the beginner than to the fundamental revolt of every true artist who wants from the very beginning to clear the terrain that he intends to cover. And since he never manages to do so without justifying himself by means of some previous example, we should not be surprised that the guides that Paul Delvaux chooses are precisely those who, in his time and in his country, have rejected academism, conventional subjects, the so-called great tradition in painting. Before he finds himself, he borrows the expressionist brush of Permeke and Gustave de Smet, the profuse palette of James Ensor.

The first canvas that he is willing to claim as his own, "The Couple," painted in 1929, reveals these influences, both by its heavy coloring and by the realism of the figures: two nude adolescents side by side. We can nonetheless discern the distant stance the young painter is going to assume, both as regards the subject and as regards his masters. It is not so much a couple that he shows us as it is two matching solitudes, and already there is an admirably *distraught* look in the young girl's eyes.

She is not yet that young woman whose effigy Paul Delvaux is going to reproduce tirelessly—a multiple image of what haunting preoccupation or what frustrated desire?—at once a horn of plenty and a prey impossible to grasp, unattainable, except perhaps in another world that she both opens to him and refuses him in an ambiguous gesture. A guardian of forbidden places where a happiness of which she is the promise comes into being, in her cruel virginity or the glory of her charms she is also their vestal. Of the fire that gives her flesh the milky transparency of opals, she makes a solitary brazier, or one limited to other individuals of her sex. The male here is no more than a back in a suit coat, a ridiculous reader of daily newspapers, an egghead with glasses, a cold statue of Adonis: blind to beauty, to grace, to the charms of life. All the beauty in the world is offered only to those who from the beginning know how to see it and to admire it.

In Paul Delvaux there is an obsession with flesh that we might be tempted to pass off as gratuitous. It probably goes back to childhood fantasies subject to strong censorship. We know how risky Freudian explanations can be. Nonetheless, how can we dismiss the indications given us by biographers of Delvaux, who picture him as a grown man, an artist in full possession of his talent, a teacher even (he was a professor at the École Nationale de la Cambre), and as passive in the face of others' force of will, as timid and uncommunicative as he had been as a child? "He bows his head like a child being scolded, sits in the place he's been told to, eats what is given him, dresses in the clothes that have been cut out for him." This indifference to the external world is not disinterest. On the contrary, he takes everything for his painting from this world, but the game that he gets on with is all inside him. It is a precious piece of information to hear a witness of his adolescence affirm that Delvaux was "made permanently a child by his mother." At the age when sexual desires are the most difficult to curb, he confines himself to a chastity that is absolute, exacerbated, and torturing. He fears women; he especially fears his mother. Women resemble her, and he respects her. What happens when this adored, obeyed, and respected mother dies, on December 31, 1932? Paul Delvaux explodes.

He first decamps, travels in France, in Italy. At one time he scoffed at Picasso, and didn't much like the painting of René Magritte, his compatriot. Now he looks at things differently. He discovers surrealism in France. In Italy, Chirico's canvases strike him as "revelations": in some obscure way he had been searching for these Greco-Roman structures, these violent removals to a strange place, these strange encounters, this "metaphysical" atmosphere in which the great painter that Chirico was always said more than he meant to, as if some good genie were guiding his hand. Paul Delvaux—the creator of an already abundant body of work, which was already "liberating" insofar as it had given form to desires and obsessions that do not belong only to the painter—at thirty-nine years of age is born to himself. He will not feel the need to formally associate himself with surrealist groups, either Belgian or French, but surrealism, by the very fact of its existence, by its poetic and graphic discoveries, allows Delvaux to progress along what he discovers to be his own pathway. He took for guides the frustrated desires of his childhood, his dreams, his solitary hallucinations, a subconsciousness too long repressed not to explode the framework of any and every sort of esthetic. His obsessive world is peopled with haunted creatures, and if its atmosphere is strange, it is not so much by virtue of a deliberate will as by virtue of a surrender to what André Breton has called "the inner model": projected all the more faithfully on canvas or on paper as the painter offers less resistance to the dictates of inspiration and submits to its orders. This man, whom his biographers describe as alien to an external world that he considered "hostile and destructive" and who deliberately shut himself up in his dreams, in this case constitutes an ideal *medium*.

As regards a thorough knowledge of graphics or technique, he knows enough so that the phases in which the work is actually done do not stand in the way of the flow of what he has to say. Leaving to others the daring deeds that "revolutionize" painting, he gives proof of a greater daring by creating the only language capable of materializing his vision and making it communicable. Moreover, between what he puts on view and the eye of the viewer, there are none of those obstacles which make deciphering necessary before the work can be understood. In a canvas or a drawing by Delvaux, everything can be seen at first glance: everything is clear, obvious, inescapable. Where does the mystery lie? In what we discover in a second look that this time does not come by way of our eyes. The look of the child that we have been, that of the dreamer that we sometimes are, that of the builder of those castles in Spain that life hurries to undermine and carry away, that of every man for whom reality cannot be limited by the walls of the useful, the possible, the reasonable. The most surprising of journeys leads us to fairyland.

A grotto in a desert strewn with stones. In this grotto a 1900 mirror with a serpentine of lace hung on it. In front of this mirror a young woman, naked to the waist. In this "Woman at the Mirror" we recognize an answer that is the contemporary of numerous "Women at Their Toilets." We are even more struck by the naïve use of a certain surrealist arsenal. Delvaux is present, however, in this canvas after the great turning point: the pensive look of the young woman is not directed toward its reflection, it is this reflection that contemplates her. Life has passed into the mirror, onto the side of the object.

On the other hand, this transmutation of the elements whereby Delvaux's young women are often only statues of flesh makes palpitate with life what for other painters would have only the barest importance as a background. The Greco-Roman perspectives, the arcades, the Italian gardens, the imaginary cities outlined on the horizon are not there to fill out the painting. Without giving it the terrifying atmosphere of Chirico's canvases, they distill this icy air that suspends the gestures and sometimes even the breathing of the figures. It is the atmosphere of a dead star, of a world beyond all known worlds, one where it is no more permitted to fear than it is to hope. Far from the tumult of men, there is no one to see, or even perceive, the existence of the forms that evolve here, all by themselves, in harmoniously composed groups or else in long processions of similar figures whose infinite progression borders on immobility. Outside of any and every presence capable of peopling their empty gaze, of giving their eyes the least reflection of the passion that they bear within themselves, these creatures of paradise are related to the most hideous hell: that of solitude, of a life without an object. They couple, mouth to mouth, breast to breast, entwining one or another of their limbs in vain; their look directed desperately elsewhere proclaims the impossibility of any sort of communication between humans. The wager here made by Paul Delvaux is that he can set before our eyes the spectacle of a chaste eroticism.

Nonetheless, these vestals happen sometimes to hold a very middle-class lamp up to their bodies, an ersatz of heat and light whose phallic meaning is inescapable, and they come strangely to life the moment that an element of the décor of every day breaches their universe outside of time. Let a Walloon house of reddish bricks stand out against a Palladian temple, let a woman in a tight skirt and an old-fashioned corset appear to make her way, rose in hand, toward a snow statue sitting on a ridiculous parlor chair, or better still, let a suburban train bursting into a picture serve as a strange background to the scene—and a curious thaw takes place.

This universe of unexpected elements, whose conjunction defies logic and good sense, paradoxically makes us rediscover a country we know, a familiar land, where time and space doubtless obey other laws than ours, but where the poses, the attitudes, the situations refer back to the human. It even happens sometimes that real dramas unfold before our eyes. They are doubtless titled "The Farewell" or "Abandonment" and once again show us the lack of understanding between the sexes, the impossibility of love. But at least we are allowed to think that there has been commerce between hearts and souls, a drawing together of bodies, a victory, however ephemeral, over loneliness. These women who, in their 1900 hats and furbelows, walk down a street at night offering their naked bosoms to the moonlight, these women who, with their thighs parted or their hands weighing their breasts, are preparing to receive the travelers of the "Night Train" in a hotel parlor, even if they represent creatures of our dreams are nonetheless flesh and blood creatures, and their black fleece, instead of being pinned to their bodies like an incongruous flower, attests that they are alive and ready for pleasure. We must look more closely to notice that the night train has departed, ironically displaying its red lantern, without leaving a single traveler on the platform, or that this superb body, in a languorous, lascivious pose, is contemplated by a dressmaker's dummy. Come down to earth from their Elysian fields where they were bored to death at the solitary spectacle of their charms, Delvaux's young women have tasted only the illusion of earthly love. The lover has not come, or he is already gone, leaving behind a recumbent victim. Elsewhere, his passage is marked by a heartbroken gesture at the corner of a window.

What constitutes the singular pleasure of contemplating these quasi-symbolic scenes of waiting that is unrewarded, of love that is scorned, of the eternal absence of the Other? What is the source of the poignant satisfaction we feel on roaming the somnambulistic landscapes in which the painter overtly calls upon his childhood memories, evokes his personal folklore of streets, railway stations, the forests and the hills of the Walloon countryside, in minute detail? It is because beyond frustrated desires, beyond the separation of beings and their mutual lack of understanding, there is a nocturnal domain where humans meet once again, and the pleasure provided by Delvaux's work stems from the obvious need we have to lay down the burden of our waking life and hasten to the endlessly postponed rendezvous that one day—long ago—we set with ourselves. Though they are not ours, we nonetheless recognize these streets, these railway stations, these hills. In dreams, we have undressed these women with the heavy breasts and the lost look in their eyes, and would like to boast of having caressed them at the time when their intimidating beauty, long contemplated, sufficed to make us happy. We have seen them push the door of our bedroom open when we were adolescents, we have met them naked in the moonlight, we have imagined them waiting for us in the main hall of a railway station. We never dared to make the gesture that would have made them come down from their pedestals, preferring to meet them, in their untouched whiteness, at the next station of the dream. Thanks to Paul Delvaux, we may believe that they are waiting there for us still.

The quest of the painter is ours, and if the magician has made time stand still, it is in order that we may answer his call entirely at our leisure. But it is time to make up our minds. After his long wanderings, ever the same and ever begun anew, the dreamer has won the right to say to the ordinary man: you do not deserve to live if you refuse both love and life. Here below is your share of what is impossible.

—Maurice Nadeau

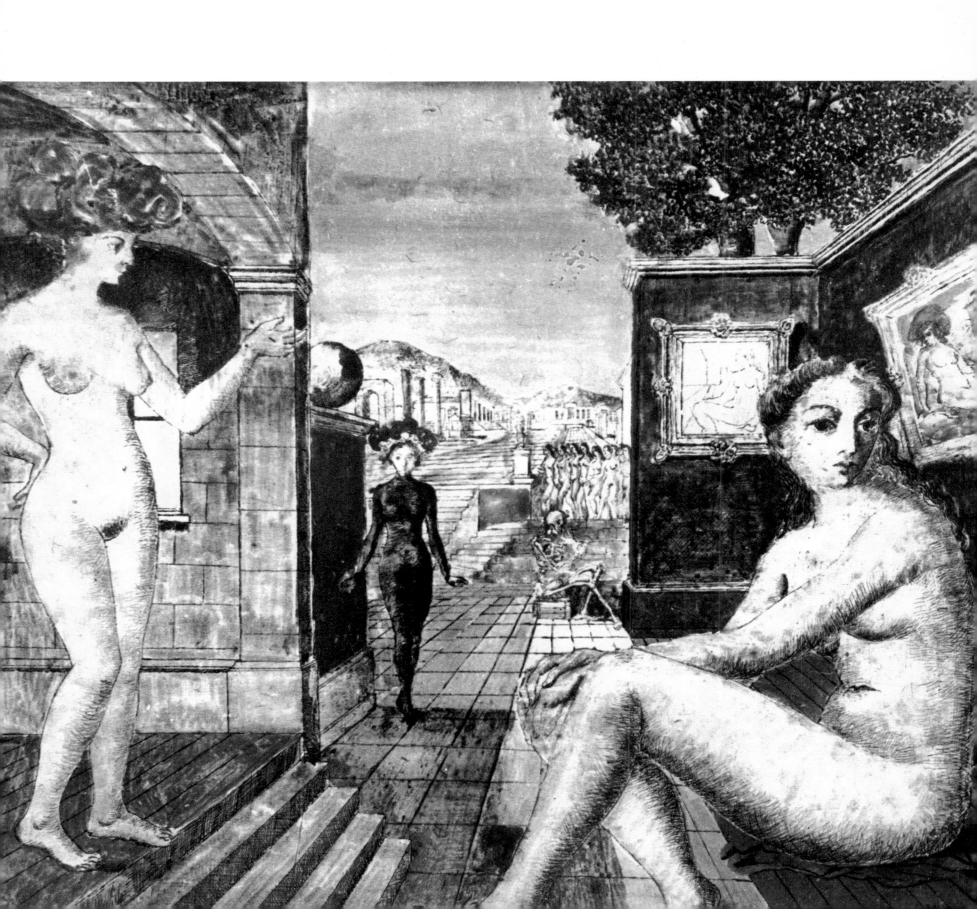

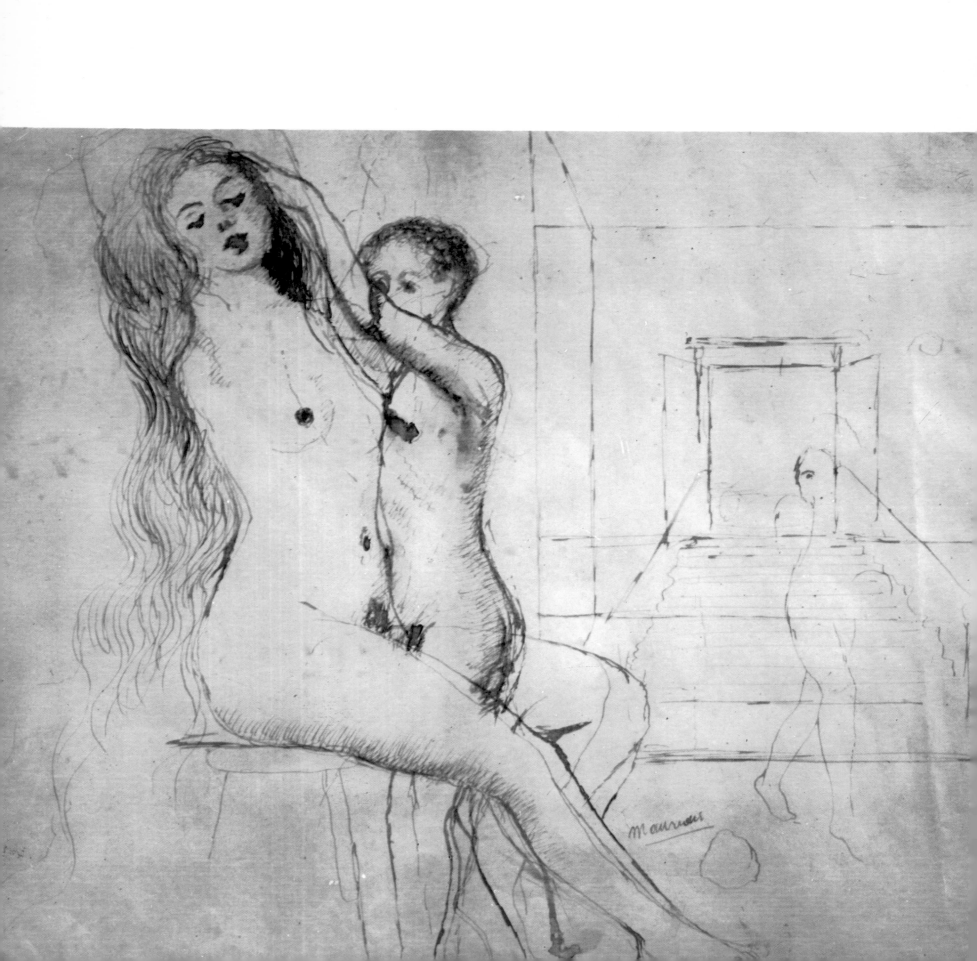

29

30

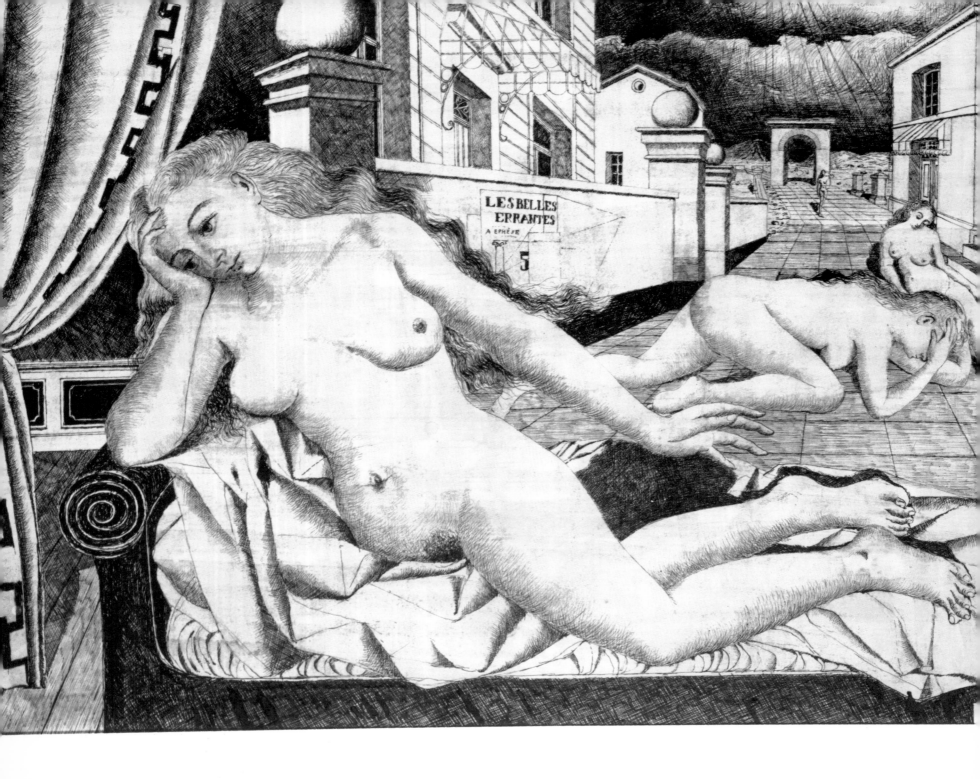

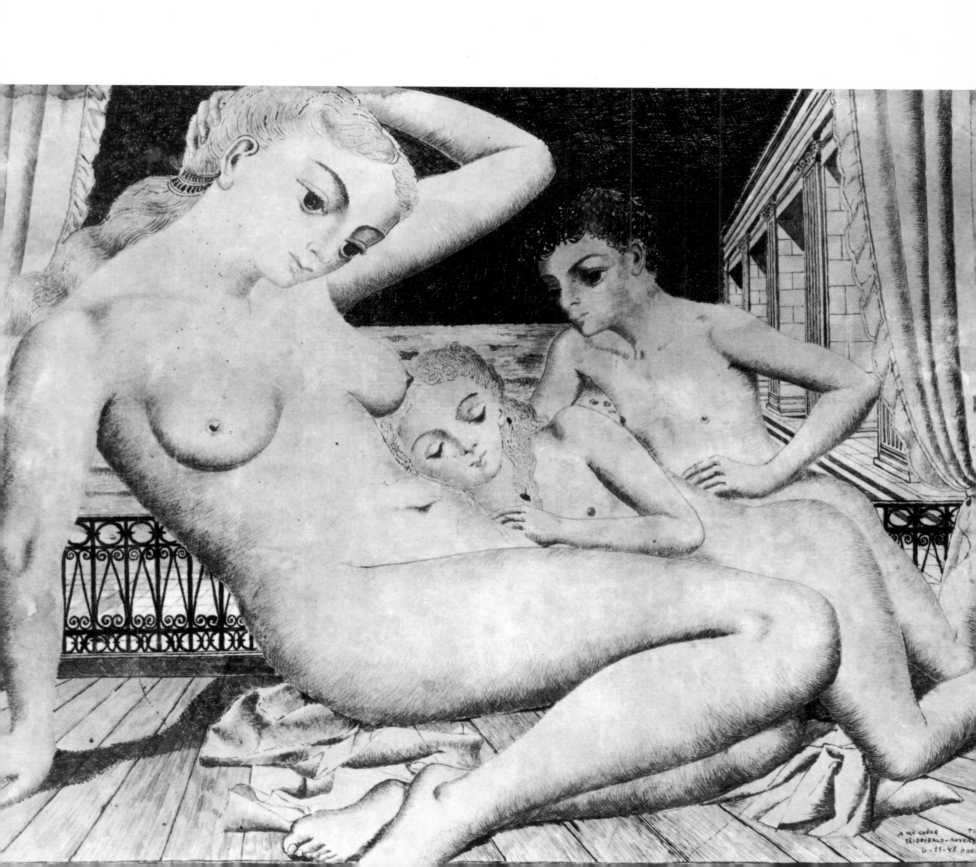

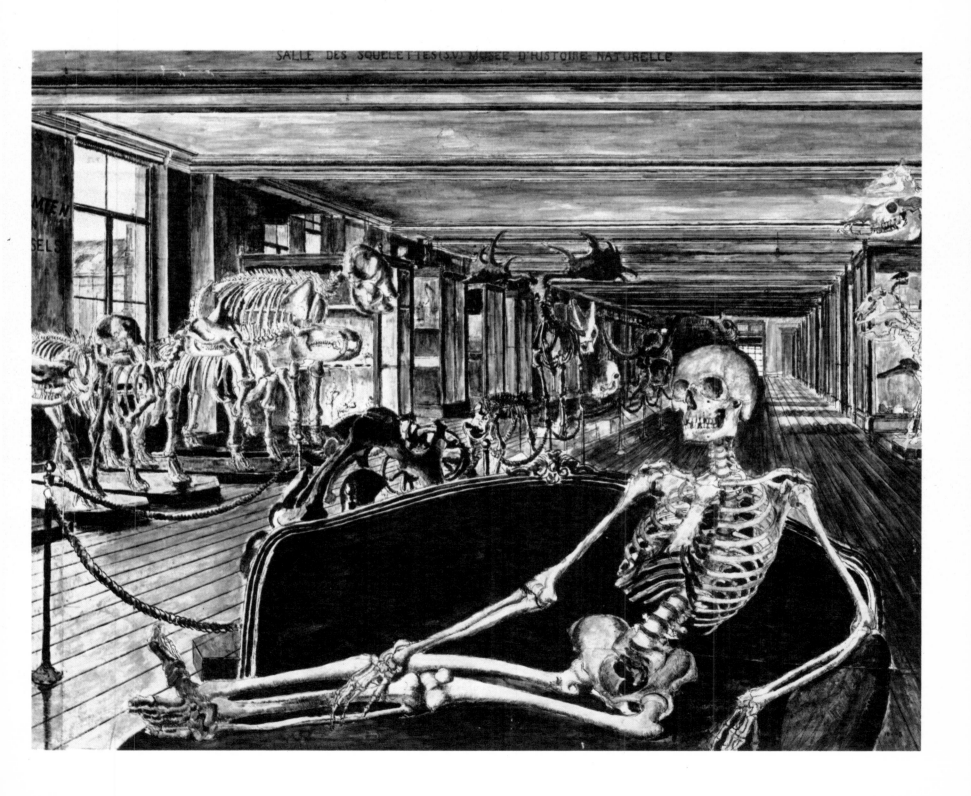

46

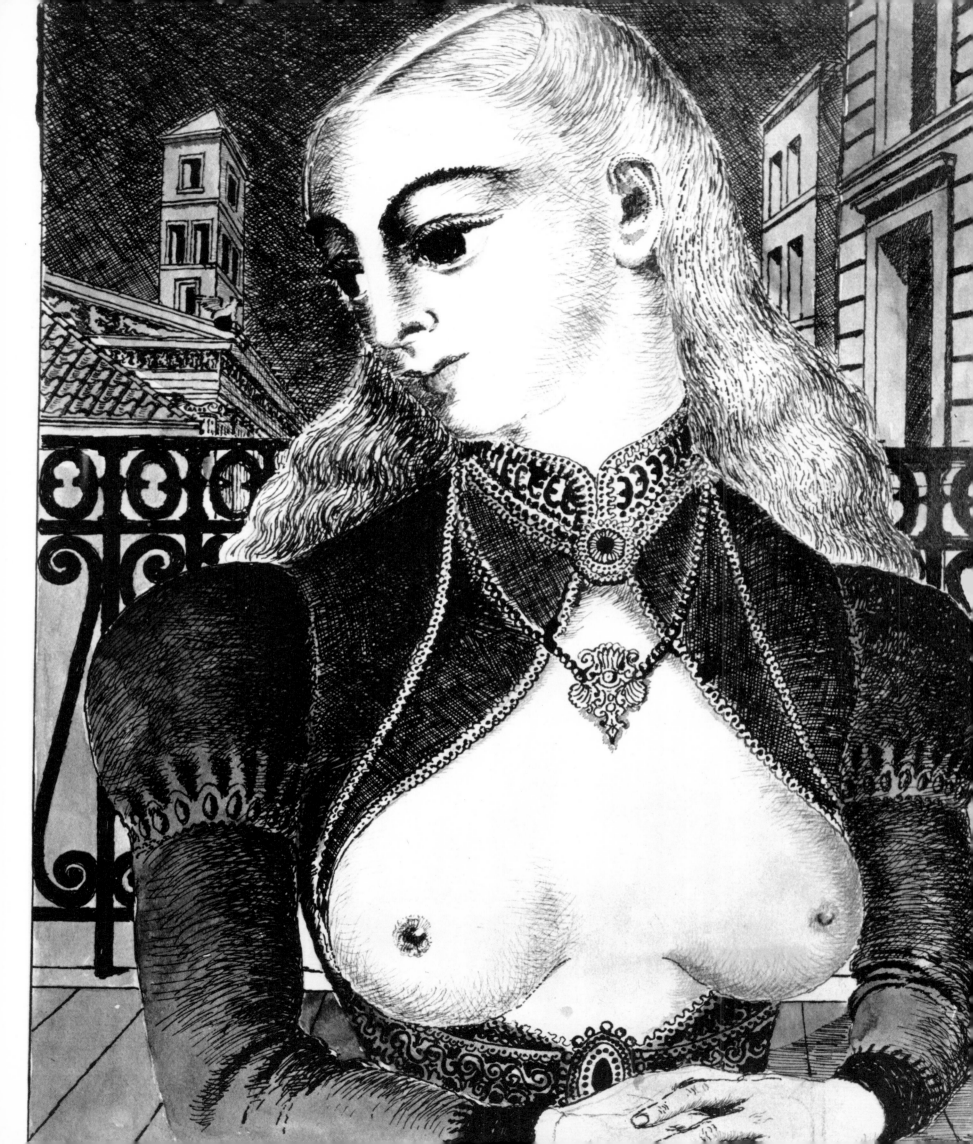

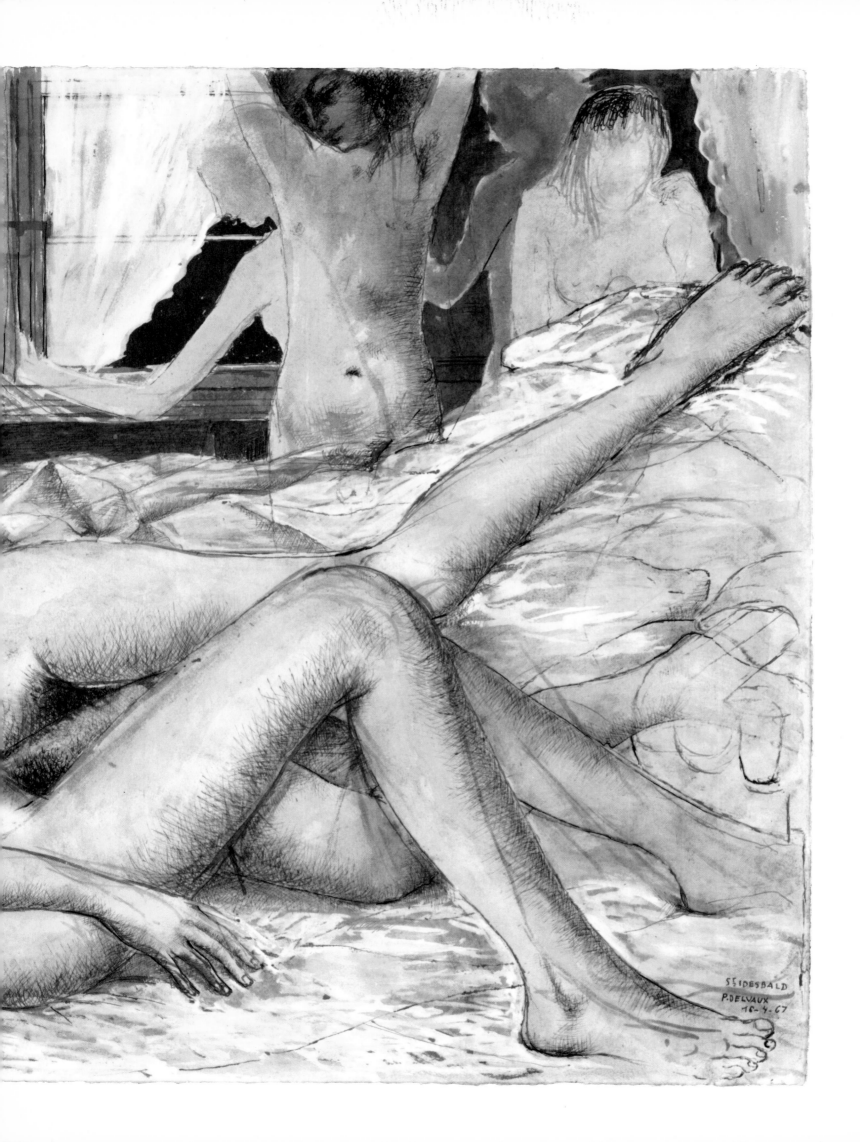

94

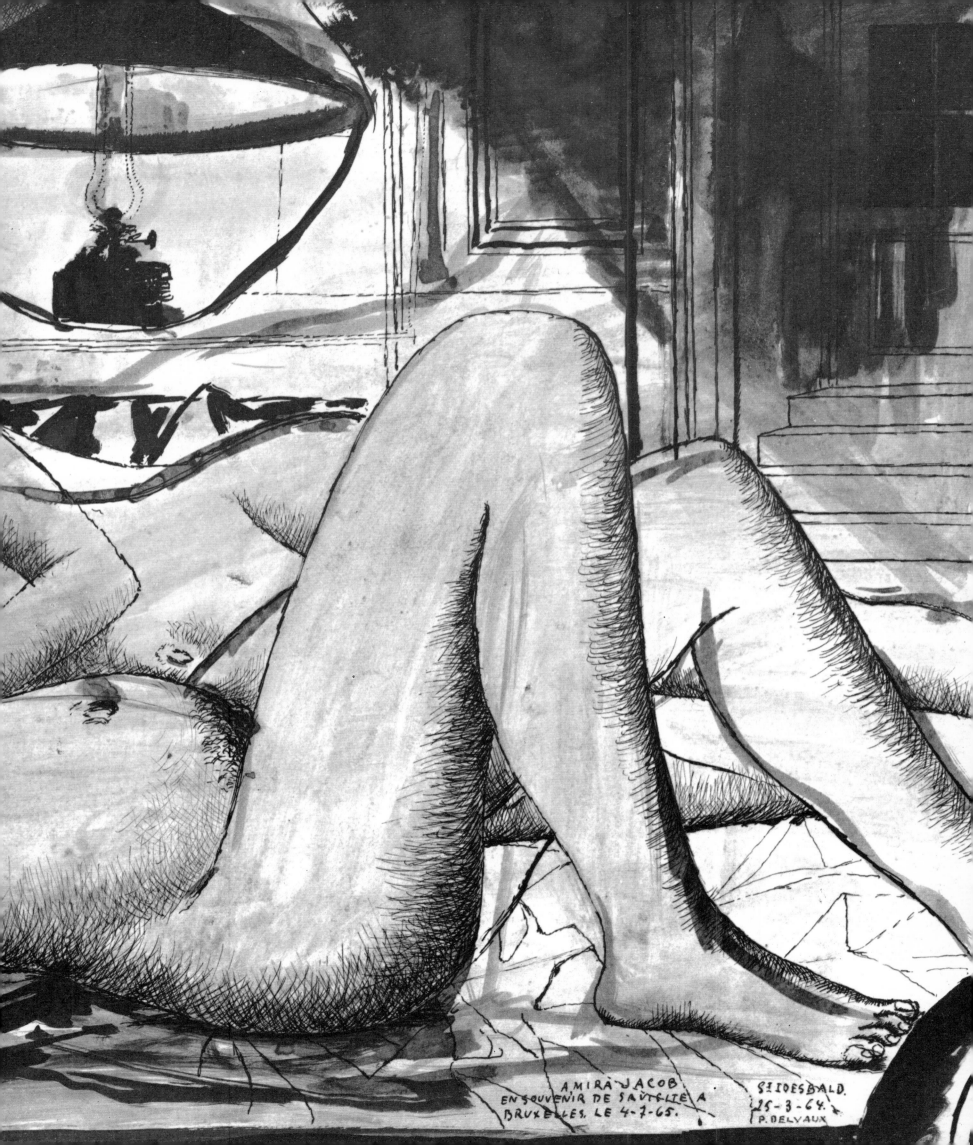

A MIRÀ JACOB
EN SOUVENIR DE SA VISITE À
BRUXELLES. LE 4-7-65.

S¹ IDESBALD.
25-3-64.
P. DELVAUX

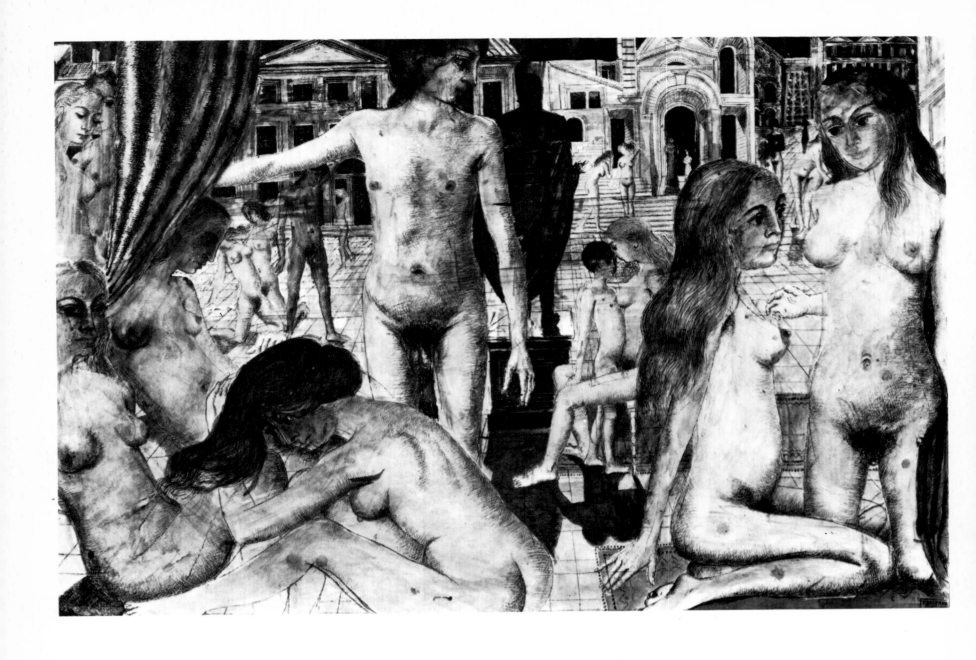

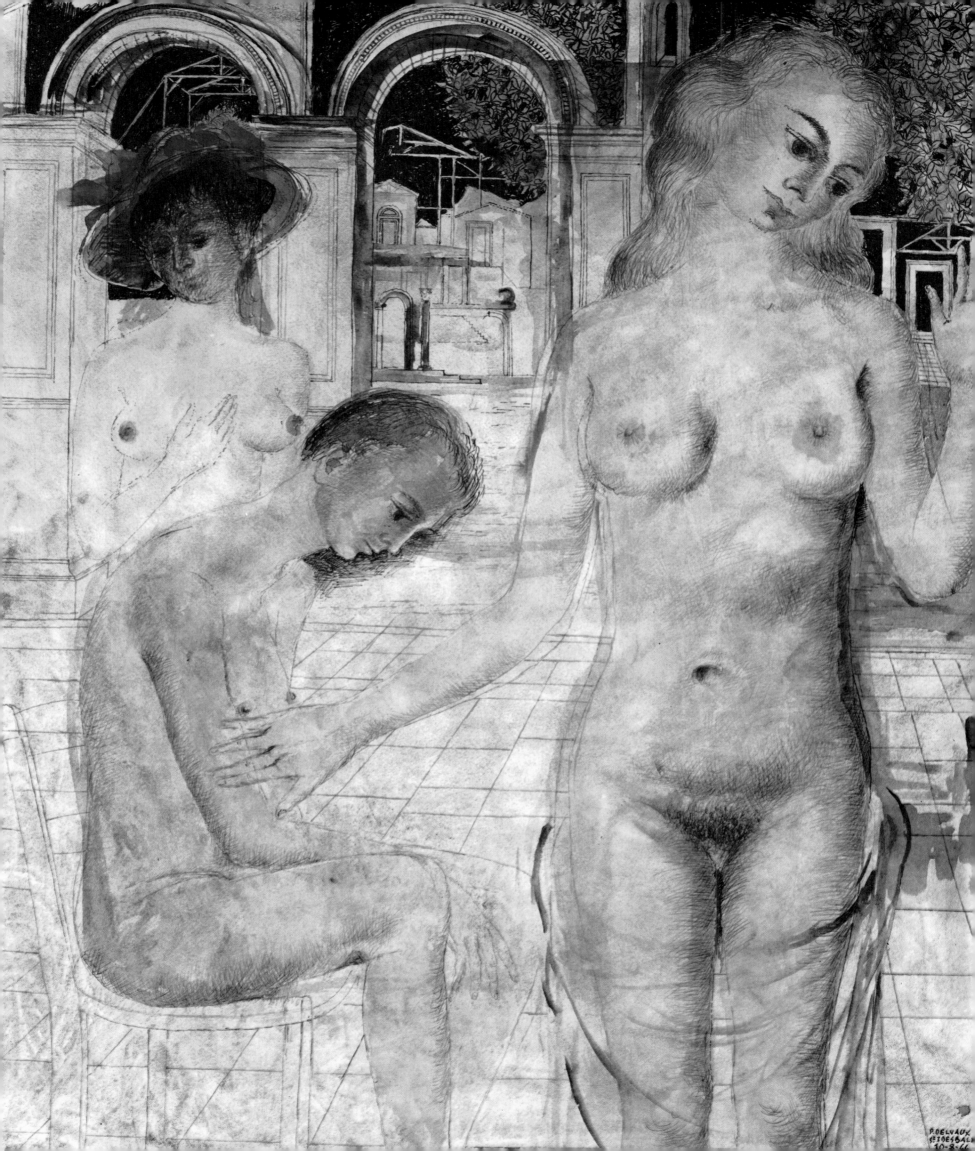

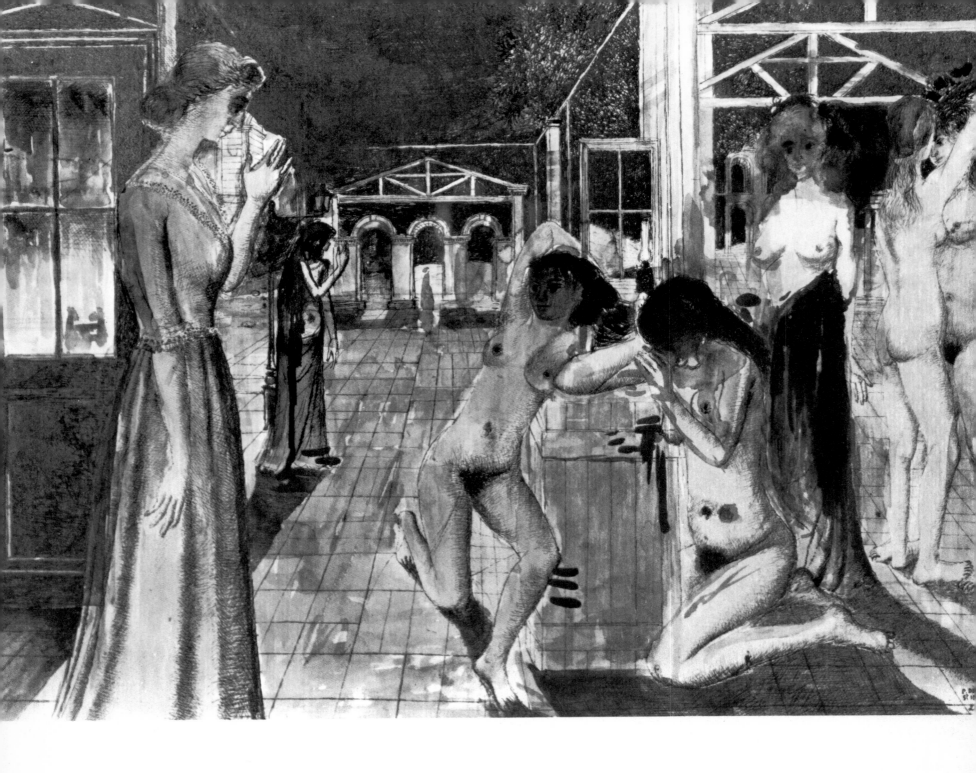

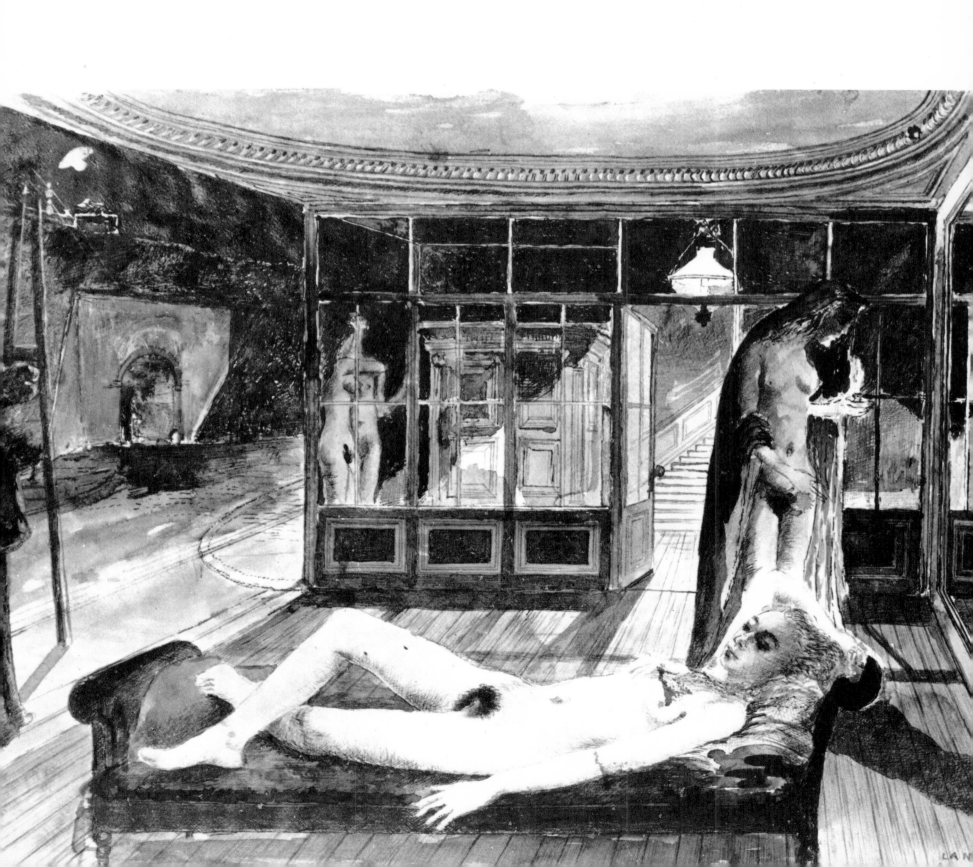

6-6-67

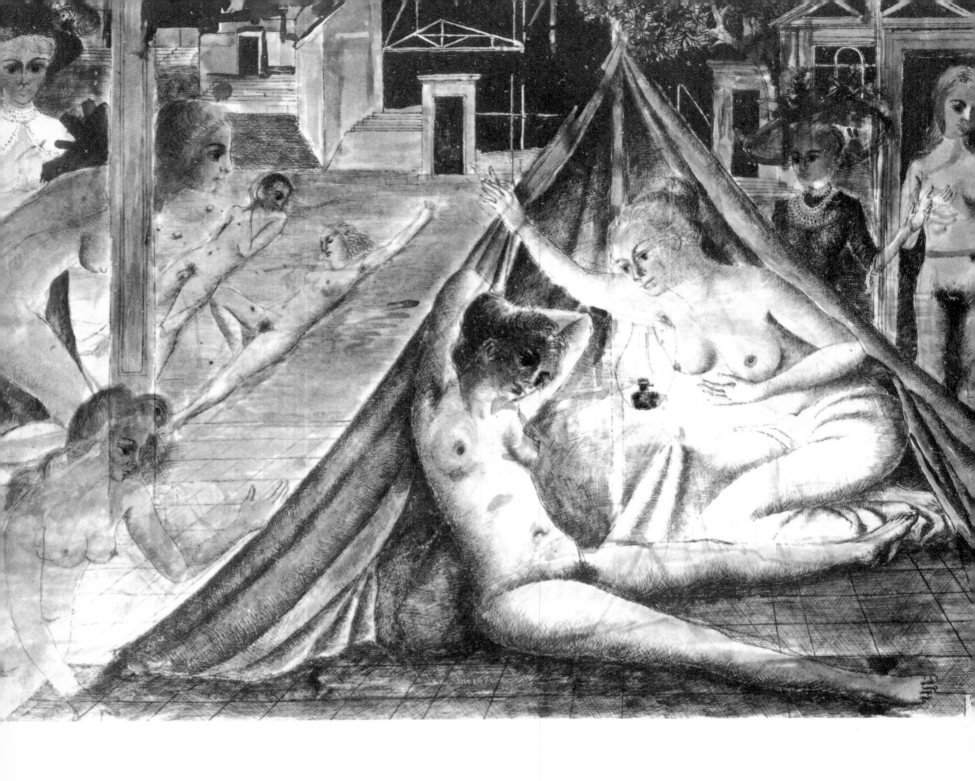

28-2-67

List of Illustrations

Some of these reproductions were made possible
by the kind cooperation of
Frans Claes and Paul Bijtebier

DATE DUE